The Issue That Challenges Every Life

Mount Everest could not be ignored forever.

Sooner or later, man had to challenge it. And the best reason that he can give for doing so is, "Because it is there!"

The subject of divine healing is the Mount Everest that sooner or later challenges every life. It needs to be studied objectively. Inasmuch as total objectivity is probably impossible, we can only endeavor to be as honest as we can—to lay aside our prejudices and look this mountain over. It may be that we won't ever want to climb it, but how shall we know if we don't look at it?

—BILL POPEJOY

The Case
For Divine Healing

Bill Popejoy

**GOSPEL PUBLISHING HOUSE
SPRINGFIELD, MISSOURI**

02-0478

© 1976 by the Gospel Publishing House, Springfield, Missouri 65802. All rights reserved. No part of this book may be reproduced, stored in a retrieval system, or transmitted in any form or by any means, electronic, mechanical, photocopy, recording, or otherwise without the prior permission of the copyright holder. Printed in the United States of America. Library of Congress Catalog Card Number: 75-43155, ISBN 0-88243-478-0.

Contents

1 The Challenge 7

2 The Final Authority 10

3 Let Us Reason 13

4 Is It Reasonable? 17

5 Whence Sickness? 21

6 Let's Talk About Jesus 26

7 Why Should God Heal the Sick? 31

8 It Is God's Nature to Heal 35

9 The Defense Rests 39

10 Divine Healing: Babel or Bethel? 45

11 Are All Healed? 49

12 Wilt Thou Be Made Whole? 56

1

The Challenge

Mount Everest could not be ignored forever. Once that peak in the Himalayas was discovered to be the loftiest terrain on this planet, man simply *had* no choice. Succeed or fail, he had to try.

Why? Because there is an innate quest within man —a quest that must respond to a genuine challenge. He may turn his head for a while; he may reason against any attempt to venture where man has never walked; he may prove to his head that climbing mountains is ridiculous, expensive, and dangerous. But proving an idea to the head and proving it to the heart are two different matters!

Sooner or later, man had to challenge Mount Everest. And the best reason that he can give for doing so is, "Because it is there!"

Now, Mount Everest doesn't bother me. I've never seen it. Furthermore, I belong to a race of beings that has seen it, and conquered it. Somebody stood on top, and—in a way—I shared his triumph.

But there is another challenge, which is greater than that snow-covered peak on the other side of the world. It is a challenge that each of us must face for himself. Sooner or later the confrontation will be there. We will face a mountain. And we will make a decision.

We may pretend the mountain isn't there. We may call it a mirage. We may turn our head and act as though we never saw it. We may close our eyes and try to forget it. We may gaze at it in wonder—firmly convinced that it is majestic but unattainable. We may count the cost of climbing and decide against it (but we will always wonder if we made the right decision, and will dream of standing in triumph in that place of lofty grandeur). We may try and fail— we simply don't have the "stuff" for such a venture. We may try, and die in the attempt. Or we may try, and succeed!

But we *will* make a decision!

I speak of the mountain of the subject of divine healing. Note carefully: divine healing is not the mountain—the *subject* of divine healing is the Mount Everest that sooner or later challenges every life. It is unavoidable, and it is undeniable. Oh, we may deny the *fact* of divine healing, but we cannot deny the confrontation with the *subject* of healing by faith in the power of God.

If we do not understand this distinction well, it will be impossible to be fair. For some might already protest, "Your analogy is faulty! You cannot compare divine healing with Mount Everest! That mountain exists, and so-called 'divine healing' doesn't!"

All right. Suppose there is no such thing as "divine healing," but there is a *subject* of divine healing. And that is the whole point of our discussion.

You may go through life without ever being anointed with oil, as the elders of the church pray for your healing. You may go through life without ever allowing believers to "lay hands" on you for your recovery from sickness. You may go through life without ever hearing a sermon on God's ability and willingness to perform miracles in human bodies.

But you cannot go through life without being challenged by the *subject* of divine healing! The thought will come to your mind. The subject is there. It exists. And you *must* make some kind of decision about it.

Shall we call it a mirage? Shall we pretend we never saw it? Shall we close our eyes and hope it will go away? Shall we concede to its grandeur while we conclude that it is as unattainable as Orion? Shall we, without any preparation, start the ascent—climbing Mount Everest in tennis shoes?

Or shall we search and see whether these things be so?

The subject of divine healing needs to be studied objectively. Inasmuch as total objectivity is probably impossible, we can only endeavor to be as honest as we can—to lay aside our prejudices and look this mountain over. It may be that we won't ever want to climb it, but how shall we know if we don't look at it?

I am not being fair, either with the Bible or with myself, if I say, "O.K., I'll look it over. But I'll tell you right now, I don't like mountain climbing—never have, and never will! Nothing you can say or do will change my mind. But I'll look it over."

Some people do not *want* to believe in divine healing. Their logic escapes me. But they are so thoroughly convinced that "faith healing" is not of God that they refuse to be convinced. They have met the challenge with unfounded faith.

Let's look at the mountain honestly. Then we can make our decision as it should be made—in the light of the Word of God.

2

The Final Authority

It is said that a group of ancient philosophers spent many weeks seeking—by means of reason, logic, and deduction—the answer to this question: "How many teeth are in a horse's mouth?" When one freshman philosopher finally suggested that they open a horse's mouth and count the teeth, he was excommunicated from their elite society!

The humor of that bit of history disappears when we consider how, in the matter of divine healing, many religious people continue to follow the example of the philosophers: they refuse to look in the horse's mouth. Their reasoning is akin to that of the little motto which states, "My mind is made up—please don't confuse me with the facts!"

Every important opinion ought to be the result of a decision made after a proper period of searching honestly for the facts. And in searching honestly for the facts, *there must be a final source of truth.* If you want to know how to spell a word, check with a dictionary. If you want to know how many trout you are allowed to catch in a single day, check with an up-to-date fish and game manual for your state. If you want to know a phone number, look in the telephone book.

You don't ordinarily check on airplane schedules at the corner grocer. A cookbook will not tell you how to fix the carburetor in your car. Jewelers don't run ads on apples. Mechanics don't operate on cancer patients. And you don't go to an atheist for the complete facts about the existence of God!

The simple truth is: for each category of truth, there is a final source of authority.

And meaningful discussion of the subject of divine healing can take place only after a final source of authority has been agreed upon. Failure to proceed on this principle leads many discussions about the miraculous into utter chaos. Impasse after impasse finally brings the search for truth to an untimely end —simply because no ground rules were laid, no single point of absolute authority was agreed upon.

All this may souud utterly elementary, but as we proceed you will see how important it is. Without it, we would be like two captains on the same ship— disagreeing over the location of the North Star!

Basically, all who discuss the matter of divine healing predicate their opinions on one of three reference points: *experiences, traditions,* or *Scriptures*. And we are going to have to settle our minds on one of the three as final authority. Until we do, we will try to sail through stormy waters by following three Pole Stars!

1. First, let us establish the fact that *experiences* are no valid proof of divine healing. They never were—either in New Testament days, or today—and they never were intended to be. This sounds redundant, but it will be proven: *divine healing does not prove divine healing.*

Yet, many books written about this subject are basically books about experiences. Now we do indeed rejoice with those that rejoice. When anyone is instantly and supernaturally delivered from affliction we are happy for the good that has come their way. If their healing is genuine, we have no cause for questioning it.

But if the subject of divine healing were to be decided on the basis of experiences, we would be in a gigantic quandary. While I know many who have been healed by faith in the power of God—and I myself have been the recipient of the miraculous touch of the Lord several times—it is also an undeniable fact that many have not been healed. If one man's experience proves divine healing, another man's experience disproves it.

Therefore, in this book you will not read about experiences. Others may write about them, and I suppose their testimony is needed in the total spectrum of truth. I have plenty of examples to give, having been brought twice from the jaws of cancerous death. But, you see, I know of greater saints than I who have died with cancer.

The matter must be irrevocably established: experiences are neither argument for nor arguments against divine healing. We must not use them to either prove or disprove this subject. It must either stand or fall on other premises.

2. Second, *traditions* must never be the source of ultimate truth in our discussion of the subject of divine healing. Traditions are, of course, important. But they become our worst enemies when they are allowed to usurp the position of decision-makers.

Jesus was once forced to say to the Pharisees, "Thus have ye made the commandment of God of none effect by your traditions" (Matthew 15:6). The truth remains: when human traditions become the norm for Christian doctrine, the validity of God's holy Word has been questioned.

And tradition, probably more than any other single thing, keeps many of God's dear children from being able to honestly examine the Word of the Lord.

We *cannot*, we *must not*, we *will not* refer to tradition as a proof either for or against divine healing. The fact that my parents and grandparents believed in it does not authenticate it. If my parents and grandparents did not believe in it that would not invalidate it.

3. The final authority in the discussion of the subject of divine healing must be the *Scriptures*. On that basis alone will we discuss it. References to experiences and traditions will not be allowed to tip the balance of reason one way or the other.

Our attitude will attempt to approximate that of our Saviour who prayed to His Father in heaven, "Sanctify them through thy truth: thy word is truth" (John 17:17).

There will be no arrogance in our attitude when we affirm with the apostle Paul, "For what if some did not believe? shall their unbelief make the faith of God without effect? God forbid: yea, let God be true, but every man a liar" (Romans 3:3,4).

Opinions, dogmas, ideas, emotions, successes, failures—all must be tried in the test tube of God's Word. Jesus said, "Heaven and earth shall pass away; but my words shall not pass away" (Luke 21:33).

3

Let Us Reason

Our single "ground rule" has been laid: *the Bible, and the Bible alone, is our only source of truth.* God's Word must either prove or disprove the validity of the doctrine of divine healing. Ten thousand times ten thousand authenticated testimonials throughout the two millennia of Church history need not be introduced; they *prove* nothing.

If the Bible teaches divine healing, we as Christians must accept it—whether or not anyone has tried it. If the Bible either is opposed to the practice of divine healing, or is silent on the subject, we must follow its teachings explicitly and implicitly.

Now consider *reason*. Reason has often been cited as a foe of divine healing—for many philosophize the doctrine away. Then apply human logic to that which must admittedly be supernatural, and they deny its reality. Finite schemes of induction and deduction are inadequate methods for measuring infinite verities.

"Which things also we speak, not in the words which man's wisdom teacheth, but which the Holy Ghost teacheth; comparing spiritual things with spiritual. But the natural man receiveth not the things of the Spirit of God: for they are foolishness unto him: neither can he know them, because they are spiritually discerned" (1 Corinthians 2:13,14).

Trouble begins when spiritual things are compared with natural things. It's like comparing the number of inches in a mile with the number of ounces in a gallon! They are in two different categories.

Or it's like refusing to believe in an omnipotent God because His Bible tells about a man living three days and nights in the belly of a whale—human logic is never more defective! Agreed, it's impossible for a man to live in a whale's belly for three days—but if God is omnipotent, the problem disappears! An omnipotent God can do anything within the limits of love and justice.

Yet, in spite of man's puny attempts to reason away the miraculous, we still insist that reason is the ally of faith—not its foe. When spiritual things are compared with spiritual things, reason is the strongest weapon in the hands of the believer. It is no problem for a man who believes the Bible to be the inspired Word of the infinite God to also believe that Jesus rose from the dead! And anyone who believes that Jesus rose from the dead by the power of God also believes that God can heal the sick, if He so chooses. "But if the Spirit of him that raised up Jesus from the dead dwell in you, he that raised up Christ from the dead shall also quicken your mortal bodies by his Spirit that dwelleth in you" (Romans 8:11).

Natural reason asks, "But why should the Lord heal the sick? We now have completed Scriptures. We need no further proof of His deity. And besides, we have good doctors, hospitals, and medicines nowadays. It just isn't needed."

The person who reasons this way should consider the fact that his logic—whether or not there is any truth in the subject of divine healing—belies any true spirituality. If this doctrine is invalid, it will not be because he "doesn't see any need for it!"

Permit me to paraphrase God's reply to Job, when that devout man could not understand the Lord's workings. He said, "Job, when I decided to hang the world upon nothing, did I ask you what I should hang it on? When I decreed that mountain goats would live in the crags of the rocks, did I ask you where goats should live? When I put the whale in the ocean, did I ask you about the advisability of creating such a monster and putting him in such a place?"

Read the Book of Job again. On and on the Lord put question after question to the man who entertained the idea of subjecting God's wisdom to the jury of human logic.

And if God decreed divine healing to be a part of the gospel, I have no more right to question it than to cross-examine the Creator about His scheduling of the tides! If He is God, He is God! How can *I* pass judgment on the doings of the Almighty?

How many would be Christians today if we waited until we understood the *sense* to Calvary before surrendering our hearts to Jesus Christ? How many would continue to be servants of the Lord if our survival in His Church were dependent upon our comprehension of God's plan?

"O the depth of the riches both of the wisdom and knowledge of God! how unsearchable are his judgments, and his ways past finding out! For who hath known the mind of the Lord? or who hath been his counselor? or who hath first given to him, and it shall be recompensed unto him again? For of him, and through him, and to him, are all things: to whom be glory for ever. Amen" (Romans 11:33-36).

Understand this: we have not yet, in our discussion, arrived at a conclusion on this subject of divine healing. We are simply and emphatically seeking to establish the fact that our conclusion must be honest. In order for it to be so it must, *first*, be founded solely on the Bible, God's Word of truth. And *second*, it must not be ascertained by the natural reasonings of finite wisdom; it must be discovered by that reasoning which is from above—spiritual reasoning, transcendent reasoning.

The subject of divine healing does not have to be studied blindly. "Come now, and let us reason together, saith the Lord" (Isaiah 1:18). If you believe, let your faith be founded on a comparing of "spiritual things with spiritual"—sublimated reasoning, which is not contrary to human logic, but is *above* it.

As Augustine noted, "We are not to say that God is acting contrary to nature because He acts in a way that is contrary to our knowledge of nature." And Paul's advice is, "Study to show thyself approved unto God, a workman that needeth not to be ashamed, rightly dividing the word of truth" (2 Timothy 2:15).

If you do not conclude that divine healing is a valid doctrine of the Christian faith, let your judgment be based not on an examination of counterfeits or on human logic but on a spiritual interpretation of spiritual things.

Jesus said, "Heaven and earth shall pass away: but my words shall not pass away" (Luke 21:33). Transcendent reason believes Jesus, no matter what evidence may attempt to discredit any part of His ministry.

4

Is It Reasonable?

Our question is valid. Although spiritual things may not be deciphered by natural reason, natural reason should be able to see their logic. God spoke through the prophet Isaiah with a logical invitation: "Come now, and let us reason together" (Isaiah 1:18).

All Scripture is reasonable. When the sacred writings of God's Word are seen in their true focus—that is, the revelation of the divine plan for the redemption of a fallen Adamic race—every facet of them is sensible. Beware of judging only conclusions: first, examine the premises.

The most fundamental query is: Do you believe the Bible to be the divinely inspired Word of God?

If you do not, our discussion is over. We can reach only an impasse. And there is no point in discussing supernatural things without an ultimate source of truth. Our argument would be as nebulous as the old hypothetical debate of the philosophers: if a tree were to fall in a forest, and there was no creature around to hear it, would it make a noise? That riddle has been debated for months at a time—all because no ground rules were laid. The word *noise* was not first defined.

You can, however, check and see if the Bible is true. It is the most provable Book in the world. Leave the ontological, teleological, cosmological, and anthropological arguments alone. Simply try the promise of Jesus in Matthew 11:28, "Come unto me, all ye that labor and are heavy laden, and I will give you rest." Now, either that promise is true, or it isn't! Try it!

If you do believe the Bible to be the divinely inspired Word of God, we are ready to proceed. Its own claim is, "All Scripture is given by inspiration of God, and is profitable for doctrine, for reproof, for correction, for instruction in righteousness: that the man of God may be perfect, thoroughly furnished unto all good works" (2 Timothy 3:16,17).

We refuse to join the ranks of either the higher or lower critics who endeavor, in one way or another, to discredit or destroy the plain teachings of Scripture. We will study the Greek or Hebrew in a diligent search for truth, but we absolutely refuse to judge the Bible on any preconceived notion of what we think God's plan ought to be!

The Bible is the revelation of the divine plan for the redemption of this fallen Adamic race—and every line of Scripture must be considered in this light. This principle immediately invalidates human opinions, ideas, or experiences as bases for interpreting the meaning of any passage of God's Word.

For example, the New Testament is emphatic on the doctrine of justification by faith in Jesus' blood (Romans 3:20-28; Ephesians 2:8,9; Hebrews 9:14). Yet who among us will pretend to understand how the act of faith in blood shed nearly two millennia ago can forgive sins today? But when we accept this principle in the light *of the Word,* seeing it as part of the plan revealed in Scripture for the redemption of fallen man, we can easily accept it. It is reasonable.

Now, what about divine healing? Is it reasonable? That is, does it coincide with the themes and principles firmly established in the Bible? We've got to know! For we believe this Book to be divine, and its own warning is: "If any man shall add unto these things, God shall add unto him the plagues that are written in this book: and if any man shall take away from the words of the book of this prophecy, God shall take away his part out of the book of life, and out of the holy city, and from the things which are written in this book" (Revelation 22:18,19).

We are neither allowed to add divine healing to the teachings of Scripture, nor permitted to take it away! In order to determine the reasonableness—the scriptural validity or invalidity—of this doctrine of divine healing, let us ask some questions.

Did the fall affect man's physical body? Can we believe that sickness existed in the Garden of Eden before sin entered the human family? Or must we deny any connection at all between suffering and Satan?

When Jesus was on earth, what did He think about affliction, sickness, suffering, and pain? Did He ignore it? Did He explain to men that "God is working out something in your life"? Or did He have compassion on them and heal them?

Did Jesus really care about the sick? Has He changed? May we accept the divine inspiration of the scriptural claim that Jesus Christ is "the same yesterday, and today, and for ever"? (Hebrews 13:8).

Is the body of the believer important? Is it to be the temple of the Holy Ghost? Are we to glorify God in our bodies? Are we to present our bodies unto God? Or does God only care for "big" things, like the salvation of the soul?

What is the meaning of the broken bread in the Lord's Supper? Why were the stripes laid to the back of our Saviour? Does God ever show scriptural approval on sickness or affliction—indicating that it is for His glory that anyone remain sick?

Does divine healing display God's "power on earth to forgive sins"? (Mark 2:10). Does the Bible teach that once the canon of Scripture is complete, miracles of healing will no longer be needed? Or did Jesus specifically say, "Verily, verily, I say unto you, He that believeth on me, the works that I do shall he do also"? (John 14:12).

Was our Saviour talking tongue-in-cheek when He predicted, "These signs shall follow them that believe; . . . they shall lay hands on the sick, and they shall recover"? (Mark 16:17,18).

Why did James, the brother of our Lord, instruct the Church, "Is any sick among you? let him call for the elders of the church; and let them pray over him, anointing him with oil in the name of the Lord: and the prayer of faith shall save the sick, and the Lord shall raise him up; and if he have committed sins, they shall be forgiven him"? (James 5:14,15).

And why did the apostle Paul pray for the sick

(e.g., Acts 28:8,9)? What is the meaning of "the gifts of healing" which are given to the Church?

Yes, it is reasonable *in the light of Scripture* to believe in divine healing today! And God's Word must be our only basis of judgment.

We will agree that some have desecrated this glorious doctrine, lowering it to the level of crass commercialism. And we will not vindicate them in their wrong. However, two wrongs do not make a right. The uncouth antics of overzealous egoists do not excuse the unscriptural opposition to a truth that is obviously a divine provision for believers—paid for by the stripes on Jesus' back!

There *is* solid ground, and we may stand on it. It isn't necessary to go to extremes in either direction. We can, and will, examine the failures—but we will remember that ten thousand failures do not invalidate the Scriptures.

Before you throw the doctrine of divine healing on the trash heap of irrationalism, I ask you to do one thing: look long and honestly at the stripes on Jesus' back, remembering that we are saved by His death—not by His sufferings. Looking at His back, and knowing why that awful lash was laid upon Him, ponder the question: "Is divine healing reasonable?"

5

Whence Sickness?

The discovery of the cause must always precede the cure. For example, arthritis is the oldest affliction known to man—some of the mummies in Egypt had it. And yet no cure for this, the oldest of ailments, has been found! Why? Because medical science has been unable to discover its cause. In the healing of the sick, as in everything else, cause and effect are inseparably connected.

Oh, it may be possible to temporarily treat the effect. Certain medications may alleviate the pain of arthritis long enough to allow continued motion to halt the crippling effects of the affliction. But stop the pallative medicine, and the disease will speedily do its utmost damage. The cause of it was not dealt with.

In like manner, we may not engage in unbiased discussion of the subject of divine healing without first seeking to discover the cause of sickness. Otherwise we would be naively putting a Band-Aid on a cancer!

There is a direct and inescapable connection between sickness and sin. We must, however, beware lest we unscripturally assume that personal affliction is a result of personal sin. Basically, all physical affliction may be traced to one of three sources: Adam's sin, the parents' sins, or the individual's sins.

well be translated "pain." One thing is clear: pain was

There was a time when no pain had yet invaded the human family. No stretch of the imagination can conceive of the Almighty God creating even the *germ* of infirmity in Adam and Eve in the Garden of Eden. After their creation the Bible says, "And God saw every thing that he had made, and, behold, it was very good" (Genesis 1:31). If God calls something "very good," it is not sick!

Then sin entered our first parents. And with it came the first reference to pain. "Unto the woman he said, I will greatly multiply thy sorrow and thy conception; in sorrow thou shalt bring forth children" (Genesis 3:16). The word "sorrow" might equally not God's original intention for man, but man's disobedience brought it upon him as a punishment.

When sin entered the world, so did sickness. "In Adam all die" (1 Corinthians 15:22). And in that future glorious day when sin shall be ultimately and finally defeated, "there shall be no more death, neither sorrow, nor crying, neither shall there be any more pain: for the former things are passed away" (Revelation 21:4).

In the meantime, the effects of Adam's sin remain with us. Because of the transgression in the Garden, we all live in bodies that are subject to sickness, pain, and death. Our bodies are inherited from Adam, and all physical suffering may be traced to him. If sin had not entered the human family, there would be no sickness.

The cross of our Lord Jesus Christ also displays a vital relationship between sin and sickness. "Christ died for our sins according to the Scriptures (1 Corinthians 15:3). Isaiah described the reasons for His sufferings in these words: "Surely he hath borne our griefs, and carried our sorrows: yet we did esteem him stricken, smitten of God and afflicted. But he was wounded for our transgressions, he was bruised for our iniquities: the chastisement of our peace was upon him; and with his stripes we are healed" (Isaiah 53:4,5).

A careful study of the work of Christ on Calvary leads to the inescapable conclusion that sickness and suffering have their origin in sin.

It is also true that there are occasions when personal affliction is a direct result of personal sin. Venereal disease is one example. Heart trouble can sometimes be the result of uninhibited eating. There is a law that is more fixed than the orbits of the planets: "Whatsoever a man soweth, that shall he also reap" (Galatians 6:7). Many are suffering today because of either mistreatment or neglect of the body which God gave them. Go barefoot in the snow and you'll pay for it—saint or not!

Miriam, the sister of Moses, stepped out of line, assuming an authority God had not given her. She complained against the man of God, and as a punishment the Lord made Miriam "leprous, as white as snow" (Numbers 12:10). Gehazi's greed led to lies, and as a punishment the leprosy of Naaman came upon Gehazi and his descendants (2 Kings 5:27).

Specific warnings were given to God's Old Testament people in such passages as Leviticus 26:14-16 and Deuteronomy 28:15,27,28 that if they disobeyed the Word of the Lord, physical suffering would definitely come upon them. These ominous warnings of Scripture are important, for personal sin does result in personal punishment. And the total harvest may not be in the world to come!

At the same time, however, we must be just as emphatic with this truth: *all illness may not necessarily be traced to personal sin.* It may be traceable to sin, yes, but not always to the sin of the one afflicted. The finger may point either to a parent's sins or Adam's sin.

Think of Job. His "friends" accused him of sin, but they were wrong. James wrote, "Ye have heard of the patience of Job, and have seen the end of the Lord; that the Lord is very pitiful, and of tender mercy" (James 5:11). Through Job, God confounded Satan. Through Job, God proved the lie to human logic in the matter of suffering. And through Job, God vindicated His servant. Job's suffering had no connection with personal sin!

Jesus told about a rich man, and a poor man named Lazarus (Luke 16). Although the intent of this story was not to teach about suffering, there is an obvious truth here: Lazarus was the man in the right, yet he suffered, for he was full of sores—the rich man was in the wrong, yet he knew very little, if any, human suffering.

Jesus and His disciples saw a man born blind. "And his disciples asked him, saying, Master, who did sin, this man, or his parents, that he was born blind? Jesus answered, Neither hath this man sinned, nor his parents: but that the works of God should be made manifest in him" (John 9:2,3). Jesus made it clear that the blind man's misfortune could be traced neither to his own personal sin nor to the sin of his parents. Thus, if sickness came with sin, his blindness was a result of Adam's sin!

Paul had a thorn in the flesh. There is much disagreement about the meaning of this phrase, but suffice it to say that the thorn was in his flesh—and it hurt. Yet it was not occasioned by personal wrongdoing on the part of the apostle.

Our conclusions are far from ambiguous. Sometimes a saint suffers because he has sinned—sometimes he suffers when no personal sin is involved. Sometimes a wicked man prospers in body as well as in pocketbook.

Let it be clearly understood: we cannot always know the specific reasons for the specific suffering. But we can always know that pain and suffering entered this world through sin.

6

Let's Talk About Jesus

It had been a long and unusually arduous Sunday. I had preached and taught several times, traveling through three states and resting little. Finally, late at night I turned on the television in the motel room —in anticipation of trying to catch up on a day's news. But to my delight I heard gospel singing, and I sat back to enjoy an hour of spiritual refreshment.

My aspirations, however, suffered a severe setback. A man stepped behind a pulpit, opened a Bible, and for more than 30 minutes thundered a tempestuous tirade against any who have the unmitigated gall to believe in divine healing today! He openly disdained the naivete of faith in the willingness of God to perform physical miracles in our times.

His attitude was one of condescending scorn, insinuating that proponents of divine healing are so uninformed they can't tell a *rowboat* from a *destroyer*. Calling us "sign seekers," he accused us of being so immature that our "antics" border on the blasphemous. He said that we are a threat to positive New Testament Christianity!

Of course, he had a Scripture passage—or at least a part of one. It was Matthew 12:39: "But he [Jesus] answered and said unto them, An evil and adulterous generation seeketh after a sign; and there shall no sign be given to it, but the sign of the prophet Jonah." For some reason he chose to ignore such passages as Mark 16:17-20; Acts 2:22,43; 4:30; 5:12; 8:13; 14:3; Romans 15:19; 2 Corinthians 12:12; and Hebrews 2:4, every one of which emphasizes the presence, the power, the need, and the blessings resulting from the abundance of "signs" in the lives of both Jesus and His apostles, and in the lives of all who believe in Him.

The preacher's arguments against divine healing were all summed up in one blistering barrage, "There shall no sign be given!" He concluded his grandiloquence with this plea, "Let's not talk about signs—let's talk about Jesus!"

I'll go along with that—*let's talk about Jesus!* But the theme is so large: where does one begin? Peter was confronted with the same problem on the day the Church was born. And he introduced Jesus with these words: "Ye men of Israel, hear these words; Jesus of Nazareth, a man approved of God among you by miracles and wonders and signs, which God did by him in the midst of you, as ye yourselves also know" (Acts 2:22).

When that same apostle would introduce Jesus to the first New Testament Gentile congregation, the household of Cornelius, he told "how God anointed Jesus of Nazareth with the Holy Ghost and with power: who went about doing good, and healing all that were oppressed of the devil; for God was with him" (Acts 10:38).

Yes, let's talk about Jesus! But if we attempt to discuss the three or more years of His ministry on earth without talking about divine healing, we have to leave a large part out.

The very first words spoken by our Lord in His public ministry outlined the course of His work on earth, and in them He established the fact that His commission dealt with both the spiritual and the physical. Reading from Isaiah, he announced, "The Spirit of the Lord is upon me, because he hath anointed me to preach the gospel to the poor; he hath sent me to heal the broken-hearted, to preach deliverance to the captives, and recovering of sight to the blind, to set at liberty them that are bruised, to preach the acceptable year of the Lord" (Luke 4:18,19).

And when a long-imprisoned John the Baptist sent messengers to Jesus with the question, "Art thou he that should come? or look we for another?" the Bible says, "And in that same hour he [Jesus] cured many of their infirmities and plagues, and of evil spirits; and unto many that were blind he gave sight. Then Jesus answering said unto them, Go your way, and tell John what things ye have seen and heard; how that the blind see, the lame walk, the lepers are cleansed, the deaf hear, the dead are raised, to the poor the gospel is preached. And blessed is he, whosoever shall not be offended in me" (Luke 7:20-23). That great Baptist was to be convinced of the deity of Jesus by the miracles which his messengers witnessed!

Yes, let's talk about Jesus! Says Thomas Holdcroft, in his excellent book *Divine Healing: A Comparative Study*:

A total of twenty-six individual miracles of healing credited to Jesus are to be found in the Scriptures, as well as ten occasions recording the general healing of large numbers of people. His ministry dealt with a wide variety of human ailments: demon possession, sickness, disease, accident, and even death. In the recorded healings of Jesus, only Peter's mother-in-law could have been expected to recover by natural means. All others appear to have been chronic aggravated cases. In each instance, Jesus freely and frankly presented himself as an object of faith to be sincerely believed. In the face of such an impressive ministry of healing, it is truly remarkable that He could promise His disciples, "greater works than these shall ye do" (John 14:12).

In ministering to physical needs, our Lord healed by a word, by a touch, and by physical anointing; He healed near at hand and at a distance; He healed on the Sabbath; He healed both individuals and groups at large. Among the twenty-six instances of healing, there are seven cases in which a demon was cast out; on eleven occasions friends brought the sufferer; on six occasions the patient himself made an appeal; on three occasions our Lord performed the healing while at a distance. He healed seven by speaking a word; three were healed in a ceremony in which He spat and touched the patient; and in one instance He healed by effecting a gradual cure (John 4:52–"He began to amend"). At no time did Jesus use scientific or medical means to impart His healings, and while some may have been emotional and have concerned the spirit and inner being, most were obvious physical restorations.

I, as a preacher of the gospel, have no warrant for deleting a very, very large segment of Christ's work on earth from my ministry! Furthermore, I have no scriptural warrant for explaining our Lord's ministry of divine healing as mere types of spiritual truths! Nor can I accuse God's Son of ignoring His true mission on earth—that of seeking and saving the lost (Luke 19:10)—by being spiritually immature, displaying His glory by "signs" which were superfluous!

The Early Church talked about Jesus. To a lame man beside the gate Beautiful, Peter said, "In the name of Jesus Christ of Nazareth rise up and walk" (Acts 3:6). And he did! Explaining his actions to the critical religious court, Peter explained, "Be it known unto you all, and to all the people of Israel, that by the name of Jesus Christ of Nazareth, whom ye crucified, whom God raised from the dead, even by him doth this man stand here before you whole" (Acts 4:10).

When threatened, the Early Church prayed, "And

now, Lord, behold their threatenings: and grant unto thy servant, that with all boldness they may speak thy word, by stretching forth thine hand to heal; and that signs and wonders may be done by the name of thy holy child Jesus" (Acts 4:29,30).

God answered their prayer, and by the hands of the apostles were many signs and wonders wrought among the people (Acts 5:12). And when the council "had called the apostles, and beaten them, they commanded that they should not speak in the name of Jesus, and let them go. And they departed from the presence of the council, rejoicing that they were counted worthy to suffer shame for his name. And daily in the temple, and in every house, they ceased not to teach and preach Jesus Christ" (Acts 5:40-42). And miracles of healing followed—producing such joy that many turned to God.

Paul, who proclaimed "we preach Christ" (1 Corinthians 1:23), was praying for the sick and witnessing divine healing right down to the times and events recorded in the last page of the Book of Acts (27:8, 9).

Yes, let's talk about Jesus—the Jesus of Nazareth who constantly "went about doing good, and healing all that were oppressed of the devil" (Acts 10:38). Let's talk about the Jesus who is "the same yesterday, and today, and for ever" (Hebrews 13:8). Let's talk about Jesus who "went forth, and saw a great multitude, and was moved with compassion toward them, and he healed their sick" (Matthew 14:14). Let's talk about Jesus who said, "Verily, verily, I say unto you, He that believeth on me, the works that I do shall he do also" (John 14:12). Let's talk about the Jesus who promised, "These signs shall follow them that believe; . . . they shall lay hands on the sick, and they shall recover" (Mark 16:17,18). Let's talk about the Jesus who said, "And whatsoever ye shall ask in my name, that will I do, that the Father may be glorified in the Son" (John 14:13).

Let's talk about Jesus!

7

Why Should God Heal the Sick?

The premises are all in order, and they tell us much about the Almighty.

1. God exists, and He is *sovereign*—neither needing nor seeking advice from finite man. He "worketh all things after the counsel of his own will" (Ephesians 1:11). Man's inability to comprehend the workings of deity is no barrier to the divine economy—"how unsearchable are his judgments, and his ways past finding out!" (Romans 11:33). If He chooses to heal the sick, who can argue with Him? He is God!

2. God exists, and He is *omnipotent*—He has all power. "The earth is the Lord's and the fulness thereof; the world, and they that dwell therein" (Psalm 24:1). He not only created all things, He also sustains all things. He is "the God in whose hand thy breath is, and whose are all thy ways" (Daniel 5:23). "In him we live, and move, and have our being" (Acts 17:28). The Bible says, "God hath spoken once; twice have I heard this; that power belongeth unto God" (Psalm 62:11).

3. God exists, and He is *incarnate in Christ*. Jesus is "the image of the invisible God" (Colossians 1:15). And "in him dwelleth all the fulness of the Godhead bodily" (Colossians 2:9). Philip once said to Jesus,

"Lord, show us the Father, and it sufficeth us. Jesus saith unto him, Have I been so long time with you, and yet hast thou not known me, Philip? he that hath seen me hath seen the Father; and how sayest thou then, Show us the Father?" (John 14:8,9). All that man can now know about God must be discovered in Jesus Christ.

4. God exists in Christ, and He is *revealed in the Scriptures.* Let this truth be firmly established in our minds: we can know nothing about Jesus except that which is written in the Word. "For other foundation can no man lay than that is laid, which is Jesus Christ" (1 Corinthians 3:11). And we are not allowed to change that which is writen, for to do so is to "pervert the gospel of Christ. But though we, or an angel from heaven, preach any other gospel unto you than that which we have preached unto you, let him be accursed" (Galatians 1:7,8).

Now, if these four premises be true—and every Christian believes that they are—we must examine closely the life of Jesus *as revealed in Scripture* in order to know God. No warrant is given us to create a system of our own, and then proceed to squeeze Jesus into our mold. We must see Him as He is, for He does not change. He never has "stepped out of character," and He never will.

It is an undeniable fact that Jesus of Nazareth devoted a noteworthy part of His ministry on earth to healing the sick. And if Jesus is the embodiment of the invisible, sovereign, omnipotent God, the evidence is conclusive that for at least three and one-half years God performed miracles of physical healing by divine power. Furthermore, believers in the inspired Scriptures accept the authoritative statement of the Lord through His prophet, "I am the Lord, I change not" (Malachi 3:6).

The conclusion is inevitable: God is interested in healing the sick; He has the power to heal; and if He chooses to do so, who can argue with the sovereign God?

Many honest men are left, however, with one penetrating question: *but why should God heal the sick?* The Almighty inhabits eternity, and these bodies of ours are creatures of time. "The things which are seen are temporal; but the things which are not seen are eternal" (2 Corinthians 4:18). Inasmuch as "flesh and blood cannot inherit the kingdom of God" (1 Corinthians 15:50, why should the all-wise God be concerned with carcasses which are consigned to dust? Should not our heavenly Father set the example for His children by putting "first things first"?

The Bible answers these questions, listing at least two reasons that are, to some degree, within the reach of the finite rationale. This short list of two reasons for divine healing is not intended to be exhaustive, but it is conclusive. It answers satisfactorily the query of the honest doubter about the purpose of divine healing. We will attempt to examine them more thoroughly in the next two chapters. They are:

First, God heals the sick because it is His nature to do so. He is the Lord our Physician (Exodus 15:26). While on earth Jesus often healed the sick simply because He was "moved with compassion" (Matthew 14:14; 20:34; Mark 1:41; 5:19; Luke 7:13). God's nature has not changed!

Second, God heals the sick because it is an open, visible display of His "power upon earth to forgive sins" (Luke 5:24). All arguments to the effect that we no longer need miracles are based on human philosophy, and not on the Word. Just as God does not change through the centuries, man does not either. Oh, there may be a surface "wishy-washiness," but the basic urges and needs of Adam's race have not changed since the Fall. "There is no difference" (Romans 3:22). Furthermore, if Jesus said that physical miracles are a showcase of His power to perform spiritual miracles, who among us will tell Him He is mistaken?

We must beware lest we argue with the inspired Word. It is our only roadmap to heaven. And its veracity is not dependent upon our comprehension of its precepts. In fact, its very concept is that it is transcendent. The Bible is *predicated on faith* in an all-wise and loving God.

"There is a God in heaven" (Daniel 2:28), and He is amenable to no man. Yet in mercy He condescends to explain His actions in a way that we can understand. "He that hath an ear, let him hear what the Spirit saith unto the churches" (Revelation 2:29).

Let us confess, with Job, "I know that thou canst do everything, and that no thought can be withholden from thee. Who is he that hideth counsel without knowledge? Therefore have I uttered that I understood not; things too wonderful for me, which I knew not . . . I have heard of thee by the hearing of the ear: but now mine eye seeth thee: wherefore I abhor myself, and repent in dust and ashes" (Job 42:2-6).

And may our prayer be, "Teach me thy way, O Lord, and lead me in a plain path" (Psalm 27:11).

8

It Is God's Nature to Heal

God's nature is seen in His works. Inasmuch as "no man hath seen God at any time" (John 1:18), we know Him through His activities. Take, for example, the simple affirmation of Scripture: "God is love" (1 John 4:8). I am not in league with the agnostics if I ask, "How do I know that statement is true? How do I know that God is love?"

Can it be *proved* that God is love? Yes, "For scarcely for a righteous man will one die: yet peradventure for a good man some would even dare to die. But God commendeth his love toward us, in that, while we were yet sinners, Christ died for us" (Romans 5:7,8). The proof of God's love is seen at Calvary. "For God so loved the world that he gave his only begotten Son, that whosoever believeth in him should not perish, but have everlasting life" (John 3:16).

When my faith is weak, and I begin to wonder if God really cares, I return in spirit to the Cross where my Saviour died. I see the ugliness of the scene, I think of my love for my son, and I remember that God loves me so much He gave His Son to die for me! And the question is resolved: "God is love."

This truth is, to the Christian, indisputable: God's nature is seen in what He does. Such a thesis does not negate faith—it elevates it. Faith tells me that God does not change. He has no "second thoughts" about Calvary. He would do it again. For the nature of God *is what it is*, and is displayed through His actions. Inasmuch as God is infinite and I am finite, and inasmuch as the finite cannot fathom the infinite, I know the infinite God only through His workings in the realm of the finite. There I see what kind of God He is.

The transcendent must be viewed through eyes of clay! Who among us can, in actual reality, appreciate the lofty grandeur of John's metaphysical affirmation: "In the beginning was the Word, and the Word was with God, and the Word was God" (1:1)? Who can enter into fellowship with a God like that?

As a matter of fact, we all can. The infinite is seen in the finite. Read a few verses later: "And the Word was made flesh, and dwelt among us, (and we beheld his glory, the glory as of the only begotten of the Father,) full of grace and truth" (1:14). John would open one of his letters with this same revelation: "That which was from the beginning, which we have heard, which we have seen with our eyes, which we have looked upon, and our hands have handled, of the Word of life; (for the life was manifested, and we have seen it, and bear witness, and show unto you that eternal life, which was with the Father, and was manifested unto us;)" (1 John 1:1,2).

Christianity may not be compared to human philosophies, which were born in the minds of restless men. And Christianity may not be examined by human philosophies, which neither are capable of accepting the truth nor are in fact seeking it!

Christianity is the infinite, eternal, omnipotent, changeless God who is revealed only in His Son, Jesus Christ! The infinite is seen in the finite. And the message of Christianity is summed up in these words of John: "That which we have seen and heard declare we unto you" (1 John 1:3). Human logic never invented, and has no authority over, the message of the gospel. "For we have not followed cunningly devised fables, when we made known unto you the power and coming of our Lord Jesus Christ, but were eyewitnesses of his majesty" (2 Peter 1:16).

Members of the Early Church did not invent their religion—they proclaimed what they saw in Jesus, believing that "in him dwelleth all the fulness of the Godhead bodily" (Colossians 2:9). They believed that they could observe Christ's actions and see the display of God's nature!

Now, Jesus is not physically on earth anymore. He has ascended back into heaven. But His nature has not changed! He is "the same yesterday, and today, and for ever" (Hebrews 13:8). The fact that times have changed is no argument that God's nature has changed. If it was His nature to heal the sick 2,000 years ago, it is His nature to heal the sick today.

The nature of God was clearly and undeniably revealed in Exodus 15:26. God said, "I am the Lord that healeth thee." The literal reading is, "I am the Lord your Healer." The statement is not primarily about God's actions, but about His nature. He *is* the Healer of men. He put back together that which is broken. All Scripture is replete with this truth.

God is the "I am." He never changes. In the Word He declared, "I am the Lord, I change not" (Malachi 3:6).

For nearly 2,000 years Israel lived with the scriptural definition: "I am the Lord your Healer." Yet very few approximated this gospel enough to be physically healed during Old Testament times. The Word was there, but infinite promises cannot be grasped by finite minds.

Then came Jesus. He *showed* men what God is like. He demonstrated God's nature. And this was the very grandeur of our Lord's ministry on earth: He came not to usher in a new doctrine—He came to earth to show men what God has been like all along! "God really cares about you."

For this very reason the religious leaders hated Jesus: He showed the world that their theologians were not presenting a true picture of God. They, like their counterparts today, had argued that the great and sovereign God of the Universe, the Almighty Potentate who reigns over all creation, is not interested in your little headache.

But Jesus said, "Yes, He cares. And I will prove to you that He cares." So He healed their sick not merely to draw a crowd. He healed them because He cared. And He has not changed!

The religious leaders were not upset about Jesus healing the sick; that never bothered them. They were upset because He often did it on the Sabbath, and in the name of God His Father. They were all for the sick being made whole, but they were violently opposed to their neat little theological applecart being upset by the Man from Nazareth proclaiming that the God of Israel cares enough about suffering humanity to go out where they are and heal them. And Jesus was crucified because He preached that God cares.

The four Gospels demonstrate that God's nature is one of compassion. We need to answer this question honestly: "Was Jesus a hypocrite when He wept at the tomb of Lazarus?" He knew what would happen. He had already told His disciples that He would go to Lazarus and "awake him out of sleep" (John 11:11). Then why did Jesus weep? The answer to this question will tell us what God is like.

Here it is: "When Jesus therefore saw her [Mary] weeping, and the Jews also weeping which came with her, he groaned in the spirit, and was troubled, and said, Where have ye laid him? They say unto him, Lord, come and see. Jesus wept" (John 11:33-35).

This may startle you, but Jesus did not weep at the tomb of Lazarus! When He arrived at the tomb, His ministry of power began. He wept when He saw broken hearts! In so doing He showed us that the great and mighty God cares about the things that bring tears to our eyes. And He will do something about it, if we will let Him. God has not changed!

The fact that men may or may not have acted upon the scriptural truth of divine healing has nothing at all to do with its veracity. Who would dare to deny our Lord's atoning work on Calvary simply because millions of people have not taken advantage of it? Or because many have tried and failed?

Was Jesus putting on a performance when He healed the sick? Was He "playacting" when He was "moved with compassion toward them, and he healed their sick"? (Matthew 14:14). Or was He in fact manifesting the Father's nature on earth—showing men that God cares and that He wants to heal both body and soul?

The message is as pertinent today as nearly four millennia ago: "Hear, O Israel: The Lord our God is one Lord" (Deuteronomy 6:4). His nature has not changed. It cannot. He is God.

9

The Defense Rests

Jesus once asked a very pertinent question—one that we usually bypass in our mad rush to hear the conclusion of the story. And much import about the purpose of divine healing hinges on an honest answer. His question was this: "Whether is easier, to say, Thy sins be forgiven thee; or to say, Rise up and walk?" (Luke 5:23).

The occasion was the healing of a paralytic in Capernaum, where our Lord was teaching a large crowd in a private home. Four men carried their lame friend to Jesus to be healed. The crowd, however, was so great that they could not get into the house. So they went onto the roof, removed some tile, and let the stretcher right down in front of Jesus.

God deals with first things first. Jesus said to the man sick of the palsy, "Man, thy sins be forgiven thee" (Luke 5:20). Thus, with a simple statement our Lord did three things: one, He dealt with the paralytic's basic problem—sin; two, He prepared the lame man for physical healing; and three, He set the stage for the revelation of one of the divine purposes for the healing of the sick through faith in God.

When Jesus told the lame man that his sins were forgiven, "the scribes and the Pharisees began to reason, saying, Who is this which speaketh blasphemies? Who can forgive sins, but God alone? But when Jesus perceived their thoughts, he answering said unto them, What reason ye in your hearts? whether is easier to say, Thy sins be forgiven thee; or to say, Rise up and walk?" (Luke 5:21-23).

Note, Jesus did not ask, "Which is easier to *do?*" He asked, "Which is easier to *say?*" That makes a difference! Everyone knows that the forgiveness of sins is the greatest miracle available to man on earth—its grandeur transcends the healing of the body more than the sun outshines a miniature candle. But the question posed by our Lord does not weigh the significance of one miracle against another. It simply asks, "Which is easier to *say?*"

Two men stand before me. One is a sinner, and the other has no eyes. Now, if I say to the sinner, "Your sins are forgiven," can you know immediately if my words have any power in them? No. Even if the man begins to live a new and godly life, it would be impossible to prove that forgiveness came at the moment of my statement.

If, however, I say to the man who has no eyes, "Open your eyes, and see!" everyone present will instantly know if my words have authority. No preacher lays his neck on the line when he says to the sinner, "Your sins are forgiven." But if he says to the lame, "Rise up and walk," his entire ministry is predicated on the immediate response of the invalid.

Thus, it is easier to *say*, "Thy sins be forgiven thee," than to *say*, "Rise up and walk." One statement can be tested, the other cannot. Jesus knew this. And so did the scribes and Pharisees.

The question in the minds of those critics in Capernaum was concerning Jesus' authority to forgive sins. "Who can forgive sins, but God alone?" The Man from Nazareth had uttered the words, "Thy sins be forgiven thee," but who could determine the power of His utterance? To formulate the words without possessing the authority to fulfill them borders on blasphemy. And the scribes and Pharisees were quickly building up a case against Jesus—a case He could not disprove; for how does one prove that he has authority to forgive sins? Spiritual matters do not submit themselves to Aristotelian syllogisms in human deduction.

Transliterating His words, Jesus said to the critics, "So you question the authority of my words, do you?

You wonder if I'm just speaking into the air. I have forgiven this man's sins, but since you did not see his transgressions take wings and fly away, you doubt My authority. How can I prove My power to you? You will split theological hairs, and continue to confuse the people. You will introduce incidentals, and detract from My message of deliverance.

"So," the Lord continued, "let's settle this matter here and now. I ask you, is it easier to say, 'Thy sins be forgiven thee,' or to say, 'Rise up and walk'? Think about it. Which would *you* rather do in public? You know the answer—you would rather deal with the unseen than the seen. You would rather argue than work. You major in the mystical while you dodge the drudgery."

The proving ground was laid out. The lines were drawn. Here is the record: "But that ye may know that the Son of man hath power on earth to forgive sins, (he saith unto the sick of the palsy,) I say unto thee, Arise, and take up thy couch, and go into thine house. And immediately he rose up before them, and took up that whereon he lay, and departed to his own house, glorifying God" (Luke 5:24,25).

The defense rests!

If it is easier to *say*, "Thy sins be forgiven thee" than to *say*, "Rise up and walk"; and *if* Jesus can prove His power to say that which is harder to say, it is incontestable that He can also authoritatively say that which is easiest. Our Lord established the simple premise that *miracles of divine healing prove His power to forgive sins.*

The crowd accepted the evidence. The Bible says, "And they were all amazed, and they glorified God, and were filled with fear, saying, We have seen strange things today" (Luke 5:26). The Scriptures indicate that even the critics were convinced, for it says that they were *all* amazed and glorified God. They were convinced of Jesus' power to forgive sins by beholding His power to heal the sick!

All the facts remain until this day. Nothing has changed. Men are still suffering in soul and body, and are innately aware that the greatest need is the forgiveness of sins—to be right with God. Yet they fear that the promise of redemption in Christ may be a mirage. Elaborate theological arguments in support of the doctrine of justification by faith whet the appetite of the honest sinner who seeks relief from the guilt and power of sin. Yet his heart wonders, "Is this *really* true? Am I to commit my eternal soul to the blind trust in a mystical doctrine of antiquity? How can I *know* that there is a real God with enough power to prepare my soul for the world to come?"

And this is one of the reasons God heals the sick today—to prove to a critical world that He has power to forgive sins. He continues to rest His case on the same defense. "That ye may know that the Son of man hath power on earth to forgive sins." I didn't say it. Jesus said it! If you have any argument, take it to Him!

"But," some will insist, "we don't need any more proof. Jesus did it once, and that is enough for all time. He displayed His power that day in Capernaum; we have the sacred record of the miracle, and now we only need faith in the written Word."

Then why did Jesus perform *many* miracles? If one display of divine power would prove His point, why did He heal again and again? You know the answer: every man needs to see the power of God for himself! The Old Testament record reads like this: "And the people served the Lord all the days of Joshua, and all the days of the elders that outlived Joshua, who had seen all the great works of the Lord, that he did for Israel . . . and there arose another generation after them, which knew not the Lord, nor yet the works which he had done for Israel. And the children of Israel did evil in the sight of the Lord, and served Baalim" (Judges 2:7,10,11). The generation that never saw any miracles forsook the Lord! It'll happen every time!

Divine healing does not prove divine healing, nor does it call attention to itself. Divine healing is a visible display of God's power on earth to forgive sins. It stands as an indisputable testimony to the reality of God. And because its witness is so potent and so effective, Satan opposes it with every weapon at his disposal.

We must not confuse the issue. The Church does not exist to heal the sick. Nor must the miraculous deliverance of the afflicted ever become the main thrust of the efforts of believers. Our attention must never terminate in this ministry which is given to the Church.

Divine healing is a sign—not a sign of some man's faith, nor a sign of a particular gift, nor a sign of extreme devotion. Divine healing is a sign of God's power, a testimony to a wondering world that Jesus Christ cares enough to prove His authority over every enemy that tries to hurt or destroy finite man.

Thus, divine healing is not done "in a corner" (Acts 26:26). Nor is it primarily for the benefit of the sufferer. It is for the glory of God. And whenever all glory is given to Jesus, there is no limit to what He will do for the believer. When He is lifted up, men will be drawn to Him. And when they see with their eyes that He is indeed the mighty God, they will glorify Him.

10

Divine Healing: Babel or Bethel?

Babel means *confusion*. *Bethel* means *the house of God*. and never the twain should meet!

At Babel, carnal man established his own system of religion. He disdained the divine directive, preferring worldly wisdom to transcendent truth. He considered it unthinkable to surrender to a plan that was totally of God. He would show the Almightly that he could make bricks and build a tower that would reach to heaven. But his efforts ended in utter confusion.

At Bethel, Jacob lay his head on a rock and went to sleep. In a dream, he saw a ladder that reached into heaven. Angels were ascending and descending on it. And he called the name of the place Bethel—the house of God.

Divine healing is either a Babel or a Bethel to everyone who has read these pages. It either confuses you or draws you nearer to God. It either raises questions or answers questions. You see it either as a human effort to devise a doctrine or as a revelation of the character of God. It's hard to be neutral about this subject. It either thrills you or gives you cold chills.

Divine healing was the bone of contention in the religious world of Jesus' day, and it still is. The multitudes believed in the miracles of the Lord, and they followed Him. But the ecclesiastical hierarchy so despised the way divine healing was turning the world's attention away from their establishment—and toward God himself—that they could not rest until they crucified Jesus.

This leads to some questions about our Lord's ministry on earth. If He were really interested in helping fallen mankind back to God, why did He insist on doing things He knew would incur the wrath of the divinely instituted system of religion? Why was the healing of the sick so important that Jesus would continue its practice at the expense of closing apparently great and effectual doors? Would it not have been much simpler to bypass all the rancor by merely preaching the gospel of salvation rather than performing miracles that were bound to create confusion?

The undeniable fact that our Lord devoted a great deal of His ministry to healing the sick—knowing that His actions would stir up a hornet's nest of confusion in the religious world—should tell us something. *Inasmuch* as we know that "God is not the author of confusion" (1 Corinthians 14:33), and *inasmuch* as Jesus' ministry of healing caused a great deal of confusion, the conclusion is inevitable: confusion about divine healing was completely in the minds of those who opposed it!

Now, we will readily, and with shamed face, agree that some who profess to be proponents of this glorious doctrine are in fact its opponents. Having barely touched the periphery of a truth, they have acted without knowledge—creating confusion. They pronounce people healed when, in fact, there is no healing. They prey on the gullibility of the simpleminded, offering "free" gimmicks in exchange for a "gift to help keep this ministry going"! Their paraphernalia run the gamut from crosses that glow in the dark to anointed cloths to miracle billfolds!

Yes, they create confusion. Their unscriptural and mercenary antics distract honest seekers after truth. Their flagrant violations of the divine directive do discredit to the cause of Christian discipleship. Many devout students of Scripture would rather wash their hands of the whole subject of divine healing than to be thought to be in league with those knights of knavery who make a sham of scriptural truth.

However, the distortion of a doctrine does not destroy it! Else there would be no gospel to preach—none at all. Every facet of divine revelation has, at some time or other, been mutilated by mischievous minds. Church history is replete with ugly accounts of popular men who made a mockery of the Bible which they were supposed to represent. Yet the doctrines remain, strong and true, in spite of false representatives.

But admittedly there is something different about divine healing! And that difference causes turmoil. *Divine healing is a doctrine for the people.* Theologians may write elaborate dissertations on the difference between the doctrine of imputation and impartation, and only a few will be curious enough to read them—while hardly anybody will care to argue the point. Splitting theological hairs simply does not interest the man in the pew.

The Bible says of Jesus, "And the common people heard him gladly" (Mark 12:37). Why? Read the whole chapter. Our Lord put down the ecclesiastical nitpickers. He had no time for their hypothetical arguments. He knew that the people were not interested in bickering over incidentals in theology: they wanted a God who could and would help them in their day-by-day lives. So He healed their sick. He showed them where Bethel is, and they loved Him for it. Their love and loyalty were not merely the result of their sick being freed from pain; they loved Jesus because He brought to them a religion that was real. It could not be subjected to theological arguments.

Oh, the religious leaders tried. The entire ninth chapter of John gives a graphic account of their struggles to discredit the healing of a blind man. But of course they failed—the blind man had been healed, and you can't argue against a testimony like his: "One thing I know, that, whereas I was blind, now I see" (verse 25). So, in total frustration, they cast him out.

What else could they do? They could not deny the miracles. They tried to create confusion, but still the man could see. Their ingrained prejudice would not permit them simply to believe in divine healing. So they cast him out!

Such has been the pattern of avowed unbelievers until this day. "*First,* deny the miracle, if at all possible. *Second,* if the miracle cannot be denied, create confusion. Distract. Engage in peripheral religious argument. *Third,* excommunicate any who persist in believing miracles." Critics don't even want miracles near them!

Divine healing is a Bible doctrine you can lay your hands on. It does not exist out there in a metaphysical world of theory and hypothesis. Either it works or it doesn't. And church dogmas will not change it— either way. If it is unscriptural and does not work, it is a Babel of confusion. If it is scriptural, it is Bethel— the house of God.

Seldom do sick people view the subject of divine healing as a Babel. The confusion is created in the minds of professional churchmen who are unwilling, for one reason or another, to believe the Bible. Arguments of tradition and human logic take precedence over the revealed Word, and confusion is the result. It should be noted, however, that *divine healing does not cause confusion!* Confusion comes either from an unscriptural practice of this doctrine or from men's opinions of it.

Divine healing is a Bethel—a house of God. It must be. Jesus preached and practiced it. All who were healed gave glory to God, and magnified Jesus as God's Son. If the pattern has varied in any way the fault is man's, not God's. And who among us is willing to concede that man's failure disannuls the divine promise?

The facts stand firm. You can no more deny the fact of divine healing than you can deny the heat of the sun. But you can confuse the sun's intent. You can either hide from it until your body withers, or you can stay out in the sun until you blister. Either extreme is wrong.

What can you gain by an un-Christlike attitude toward divine healing? Try believing in it. You just might discover the house of God!

11

Are All Healed?

I had invited the man to come to church, but he let me know in no uncertain terms that he would not attend anybody's church. A question mark must have been written on my face, for he continued, "I'll tell you why I won't go. My mother believed in God. She was a saint if there ever was one. When she was up in years, she was stricken down with cancer. She prayed, oh, how she prayed! I remember hearing her talk to God. She really believed in Him.

"But, preacher," he said, "my mother died with cancer. And to the very day she died, she believed God would heal her. She died trusting God, and that's why I won't go to church with you or anybody else! I want nothing to do with that kind of God."

Seeing his barrier of bitterness, I simply said, "Man, I feel sorry for you. You tell me that your mother died trusting God. Can you think of a better way for her to die? I've heard people die cursing God. Yet simply because the Almighty did not cater to your carnal whim, you hate Him. Man, you've got a lot to learn, and I hope you learn it before your time comes to die!"

Puny man's arguments about the doings of the Deity remind me of two ants standing on a railroad track, arguing about the justice of trains! Philosophic attempts to dethrone the Almighty—or at least to squeeze Him into a mold where He can be managed —will not have as much effect on God's absolute sovereignty as a feather can have in holding back the tide.

Two nearly unpronounceable names, listed in Paul's letters, are the delight of all vociferous opponents of divine healing. They are Epaphroditus (Philippians 2:25-27) and Trophimus (2 Timothy 4:20). The first was sick "nigh unto death" for a while before "God had mercy on him" and he recovered. The second was so sick that Paul had to leave him at Miletus.

But since when do exceptions make the rule? Have you purchased a sundial so you can check the reliability of your clock? After all, the sun did stop once (Joshua 10:12,13)! And another time it traveled east instead of west (Isaiah 38:8)! Although both of those incidents were in contradiction to the divine promise in Genesis 8:22, they do not invalidate it.

Furthermore, are you willing to accept the scriptural accounts of Jesus' having compassion on the sick and healing them? Why, then, did He many times walk past the lame man at the gate Beautiful? And why did He single out one man to be healed at Bethesda?

There are some things in the divine economy that we do not understand.

But there are also some things in the divine economy that we *do* understand. God does care for the sick and afflicted. He has compassion on them. The stripes were laid to Jesus' back for their healing. And the prescriptions for appropriating the divine promise are explicitly outlined in the Scripture.

The choice is now ours: do we want to magnify the things we do not understand, or to magnify the things we do understand? Shall we become engrossed with the exceptions, or shall we revel in the revelation of the goodness of the God who inhabits eternity? Shall we attempt to measure the infinite by finite standards?

Paul had a thorn in the flesh (2 Corinthians 12:1-10). Bible scholars disagree as to its exact identification. But we know four things about the thorn: it was in Paul's flesh, it hurt, Paul prayed for its removal, and God left it there. I personally concur with those who identify the apostle's thorn as poor eyesight. But, regardless of that, it is important to note that Paul never became bitter over his affliction. He learned that God cares more for his soul than for his body, and that man of God had implicit trust in his Lord. He believed God.

Bear in mind, too, that Paul's personal experience never relaxed his faith in the divine will to heal the sick. Immediately upon reporting God's kindness in allowing him to have a thorn in his flesh, the apostle wrote: "In nothing am I behind the very chiefest apostles, though I be nothing. Truly the signs of an apostle were wrought among you in all patience, in signs, and wonders, and mighty deeds" (2 Corinthians 12: 11,12). Paul was not a preacher of "thorns," he was a preacher of the power of God to deliver! Even a casual glance at the record of his life will show him praying for the sick—and seeing them healed—right down to the close of the scriptural account of his days on earth.

Here, then, is the principle: unless we have a specific and undeniable revelation from God that our affliction is for a purpose, we are praying according to God's will when we seek healing. And if such a revelation is given, it should be recognized as an exception to the rule—not an annulment of it. Also, the disclosure of a higher purpose must not deter the believer from continuing to act in recognition of the fact that it *is* God's will to heal the sick. Paul, with a thorn in the flesh, preached healing and prayed for the sick. And we must never, never hold our personal experience as the norm for all believers. God's Word is the norm!

We admit it, we are talking about the exceptional experience. Very few saints are in Paul's category. In our lifetime we may never meet a child of God who has had a specific and undeniable message from God that his affliction is to remain. And although many "glory" in their "infirmities," their reasons for doing so are poles apart from Paul's.

Then, are all healed? No, they are not. They were

not in New Testament times—even during the ministry of Jesus—and they are not today. Why not? The Bible does not elaborate on the answer to this question, and any preacher who claims to have all the answers is only beating the air. He is too proud to confess his ignorance. And he has somehow concocted the theology which demands that God explain all His actions to men! What arrogance!

It is true, of course, that some causes for failure are listed in Scripture. *Unbelief* is a barrier to the miraculous (Matthew 15:58). Personal *iniquity* stops prayers from being answered (Psalm 66:18). Sometimes prayer and *fasting* are necessary (Matthew 17:21). And there are times when nothing less than *obedience* to the revealed will of God will effect the deliverance (John 9:7).

But, let's face it, there are occasions when all known conditions are met, there is no word from God, and healing does not come. Then what? Should we continue to pray for healing? When the headache hangs on for days, is it an act of unbelief to take an aspirin? If the malignancy continues to grow, is it wrong to have surgery?

Some sincere children of God have erred at this point. Without scriptural warrant, they have assumed that doctors and medicine are wrong—but there is not one verse of Scripture that condemns either!

Yes, there are verses which recognize that doctors can go so far and no farther (Luke 8:43; Mark 5:26). But there is absolutely no Scripture passage at all that condemns doctors. In fact, Jesus Christ, our Lord, explicitly said that the sick *need* a physician (Matthew 9:12)! And the Holy Spirit must have had a reason for calling Luke "the beloved physician" (Colossians 4:14), rather than dubbing him "a former physician." What a tragedy that some have died rather than put their bodies under the care of a good doctor!

What about medicine? Is it wrong? Is taking it an act of unbelief? Here again, tradition has, for many, usurped the role of law and gospel. Let's go back to the Bible! There is no Scripture passage that speaks against medicine. Twice Jeremiah declares that man's medicine cannot cure Judah's sin (Jeremiah 30:13; 46:11). And that principle applies today: you can't take a cough syrup that will cure lying! But the other two times God's Word mentions medicine—Proverbs 17:22 and Ezekiel 47:12—it is used in a very good sense.

The inspired Scriptures *do* give the record of a man advising another believer to take medicine! The two men are—of all people—Paul and Timothy! Here is the record of a letter from the apostle to his son in the Lord: "Drink no longer water, but use a little wine for thy stomach's sake and thine often infirmities" (1 Timothy 5:23). A lot of people wish that verse were not in the Bible, but it is. I have no interest at all in discussing the age of the wine, but I would have you note the intent of it. Timothy had a bad stomach, and he was sickly. And Paul prescribed some medicine—call it any other name you want, it was medicine!

Why didn't Paul pray for Timothy? Knowing what we know of Paul from the Scriptures, I'm sure he did. But Timothy was not healed. There is no indication of a revelation that God had a reason for allowing such a malady in this man of God. Nor did Paul tell his spiritual son to "take a step of faith" and throw his wine bottle away! The apostle would rather have Timothy take his medicine and spread the gospel than lie in a bed of pain and create questions about the Lord's wisdom.

Yes, I believe in divine healing. So did Paul. And until I receive incontestable word from heaven otherwise, I will pray for God to heal the sick. The fact that a man is in the hospital or that he is taking a dozen kinds of pills a day will have no effect on my faith. If God heals him, he'll be out of that bed. And he certainly doesn't take medicine because he likes its taste!

In fact, on the basis of God's Word, until healing comes the sick man *ought* to be under a doctor's care! When will we learn that divine healing is a reasonable, a sensible, doctrine?!

Yet, while I believe in divine healing, I also believe in a sovereign and omniscient God. He is under no obligation to tell us everything, and we will waste no time in quizzing him. If healing does not come, we will keep on praying—not demanding or ordering the Almighty. In the meantime we will recognize that these bodies are the temples of the Holy Ghost (1 Corinthians 6:19), and we will do everything humanly possible to keep them in good health. We will take literally the words of our Lord: "There is nothing from without a man, that entering into him can defile him" (Mark 7:15).

We will rest in the assurance that our God knows what He is doing—someday we'll understand—and we will not torture ourselves with unscriptural ideas that it's better to die trusting God than to have an operation.

Until God shows us His perfect will in the matter, we will listen to the Word of God which says, "For ye are bought with a price: therefore glorify God in your body, and in your spirit, which are God's" (1 Corinthans 6:20).

12

Wilt Thou Be Made Whole?

The fact of divine healing is no more open to debate than is the saltiness of the sea—it exists. It was a matter of record in New Testament times, and it is a matter of record today. Ten thousand phonies, charlatans, counterfeits, and swindlers actually prove rather than disprove the genuineness of healing through faith in God—did you ever see a counterfeit three-dollar bill? Pharaoh's magicians and their sorceries do not keep us from believing in the mighty miracles performed through Moses.

Mount Everest stands. If you wish, you may turn your head and deny its existence. That's your privilege. But I warn you, on the authority of God's Word, willful denial of the genuine goodness of the Lord in healing the sick and afflicted can result in total spiritual blindness! We're not bickering with you about ecclesiastical semantics. We're not seeking converts to "our side." We simply point you to Jesus, and tell you unequivocally that He is God manifest in the flesh and that He never changes.

The Lord healed a blind man. Egoistic religious leaders were only interested in the "how"; they never cared about the "why." "And Jesus said, For judgment I am come into this world, that they which see not might see; and that they which see might be made blind" (John 9:39). You fit into one category or the other right now.

And arguments will not change the facts!

So, rather than bicker over the reality of the genuine, we ask those who know God and who need healing, "Wilt thou be made whole?" Do you want to be well? How can you appropriate the promise? Is it possible to move divine healing from the cupboards of dogma onto the platter of experience? If so, how?

In answering these questions, "of making many books there is no end; and much study is a weariness of the flesh" (Ecclesiastes 12:12). Suffering humanity is told to "release your faith!"—but, so help me, I don't know what that means! You are admonished to barter with the Almighty—as though Omnipotence were in dire need of seven dollars! For a "gift of faith" you can secure a bottle of water direct from the River Jordan, a piece of cloth that was placed in Jesus' tomb, a leaf from Gethsemane, a cross that glows in the dark, some olive oil from the Holy Land, and on and on and on—idolatry itself, resurrected from the dead! You are instructed to lie—testifying that you are healed when, as a matter of fact, you are not. You are told to take ludicrous "steps of faith," running the gamut from throwing away the insulin to burning the crutches.

Absolutely none of these things have any support from Scripture! And neither is there a demon in every wart!

"Wilt thou be made whole?" I have a list of 10 things you should do. Examine the list carefully. Not one item on it can be seriously questioned by any believer in God and His Bible. You have nothing to lose, but everything to gain. Slowly, prayerfully, honestly, and humbly do these 10 things—and a miracle will happen for you.

1. *Realize who you are.* You are a child of God, a joint-heir with Christ (Romans 8:17). You are "of the household of God" (Ephesians 2:19). Your name is

written in "the book of life" (Revelation 20:15). When you pray, you say, "Our Father" (Matthew 6:9). You are a member of the body of Christ (1 Corinthians 12:13). You have been declared righteous through faith in Jesus' blood (Romans 3:24,25). Because you have been "born again" (John 3:3), "old things are passed away; behold, all things are become new" (2 Corinthians 5:17). "Behold, what manner of love the Father hath bestowed upon us, that we should be called the sons of God" (1 John 3:1).

This is important. Don't let the enemy torment you with thoughts about your past. Read Ephesians 2. God has no stepchildren! His inheritance is in His saints (Ephesians 1:18).

2. *Repent of your sins.* Every time a man begins to consider his high and holy position in Christ, personal ugliness is seen. "But why should He love me? I'm so undeserving!" We feel like Isaiah, who saw the holiness of the Lord and cried, "Woe is me! for I am undone; because I am a man of unclean lips" (Isaiah 6:5).

Then what should we do? John wrote, "My little children, these things write I unto you, that ye sin not. And if any man sin, we have an advocate with the Father, Jesus Christ the righteous" (1 John 2:1). Remember, "God resisteth the proud, and giveth grace to the humble" (1 Peter 5:5). "The sacrifices of God are a broken spirit: a broken and contrite heart, O God, thou wilt not despise" (Psalm 51:17).

Be honest with God. If you sinned, it's your fault —nobody else's! "He that covereth his sins shall not prosper: but whoso confesseth and forsaketh them shall have mercy" (Proverbs 28:13).

3. *Reckon that God is able and willing to heal you.*

Reread Matthew, Mark, Luke, and John. See what Jesus was like when He was on earth. Find, if you can, one verse of Scripture which indicates that our Lord has changed, that He is no longer either able or willing to heal his suffering saints. Don't seek arguments from human logic, from human experience, or from church dogmas. Search the Scriptures, and find your answer there.

Reread the pages of this book. I have not given experiences—although I could! I have given you the Word. Check it out for yourself. You don't need to ask any unbelieving preacher about it.

If you are unwilling to reckon that God is able and willing to heal you, there is no point in reading further. However, you should at least spend an hour contemplating the stripes on Jesus' back. Remember that He is "the same yesterday, and today, and for ever" (Hebrews 13:8).

4. *Request your healing.* Yes, it is true that "your heavenly Father knoweth that ye have need of all these things" (Matthew 6:32). Yet Jesus admonished, "Ask, and it shall be given you; seek, and ye shall find; knock, and it shall be opened unto you" (Matthew 7:7). And at the close of His earthly ministry, our Lord emphasized the pattern has not changed: "And whatsoever ye shall ask in my name, that will I do, that the Father may be glorified in the Son" (John 14:13).

James wrote, "Ye have not, because ye ask not" (4:2). And John was most emphatic of all: "And whatsoever we ask, we receive of him, because we keep his commandments, and do those things that are pleasing in his sight. . . . And this is the confidence that we have in him, that, if we ask any thing according to his will, he heareth us: and if we know that he hear us, whatsoever we ask, we know that we have the petitions that we desired of him" (1 John 3:22; 5:14,15).

Have you asked the Lord—out loud—for your healing? Maybe that's all He's waiting for!

5. *Refer all questions to your Attorney.* Don't discuss anything with the devil—that's what you have an Advocate for! Trust your Lawyer. He is handling your case well.

It is possible to become so engrossed with peripheral questions that all attention is turned away from Jesus. Feed on doubts and you will become a doubter. Feed on faith, and you will become a believer.

"But I know somebody who . . .!" Better watch out! You are on the verge of testing God's Word on the premises of someone's experience—and only God knows all the details of that particular case. "For what if some did not believe? shall their unbelief make the faith of God without effect? God forbid: yea, let God be true, but every man a liar" (Romans 3:3,4).

6. *Remember your calling.* You are a representative of Jesus Christ on earth. If you covet divine healing simply so you won't hurt any more, you probably won't get it. If you covet divine healing primarily for the purpose of pointing men to Christ, you are a candidate for a miracle.

Avoid egoism which makes everything orbit around you. "He must increase, but I must decrease" (John 3:30) is the working principle of believers. "Now then we are ambassadors for Christ" (2 Corinthians 5:20). You represent Him on earth. Quit your whining. Hold your head high. You are royalty!

And you have one assignment: "My meat is to do the will of him that sent me, and to finish his work"

(John 4:34). Answer honestly, are you an attraction to Christ while you are in chronic pain? Is that His will for you? No, remember your calling.

7. *Reflect on God's goodness.* Has He ever done you wrong? "Or what man is there of you, whom if his son ask bread, will he give him a stone? Or if he ask a fish, will he give him a serpent? If ye then, being evil, know how to give good gifts unto your children, how much more shall your Father which is in heaven give good things to them that ask him?" (Matthew 7:9-11).

Divine healing is good. The apostle Peter told "how God anointed Jesus of Nazareth with the Holy Ghost and with power: who went about doing good, and healing all that were oppressed of the devil; for God was with him" (Acts 10:38).

If you can't trust your Heavenly Father, whom can you trust?

8. *Revel in God's blessings.* To do this, you must realize that your Lord loves you and that He blesses you in countless ways that you are unaware of. Read Philippians. The letter was written from prison. The theme is, "Rejoice in the Lord alway: and again I say, Rejoice" (4:4). Hypochondriacs never get healed.

Again Paul wrote from prison, "In everything give thanks: for this is the will of God in Christ Jesus concerning you" (1 Thessalonians 5:18). Start counting your blessings. Tears will turn to triumph. Frustrations will disappear. And stumbling-stones will become stepping-stones.

9. *Rest in His care.* Worry is wrong. The God who cares for the sparrows and the flowers cares for you.

"Ye are of more value than many sparrows" (Luke 12:7) Believest thou this?

Peter was in prison. He was to be beheaded at sunrise, as James had been. An angel of God came to deliver him, and "Peter was sleeping between two soldiers, bound with two chains" (Acts 12:6)! He was resting in God's care.

Paul was in a storm at sea. The sailors had given up hope. But the apostle announced, "Wherefore, sirs, be of good cheer: for I believe God" (Acts 27:25). He was resting in God's care. "Casting all your care upon him; for he careth for you" (1 Peter 5:7).

10. *Redeem the time.* Get busy. You have no time to indulge in self-pity. Of 10 lepers it is said that "as they went, they were cleansed" (Luke 17:14). Drones receive nothing from the Lord. We are saved to serve. We walk in the footsteps of the One who said, "The Son of man is come to seek and to save that which was lost" (Luke 19:10).

Put on the whole armor of God, fight the good fight of faith, run to win, and when someone asks you about your headache, you will reply, "What headache? Who's paying attention to a headache? I'm working while it is day, for night is coming when no man can work!"

Now, have you been made whole? If you have been healed, do these two things: *one,* return to give thanks to God (Luke 17:16), and *two,* publish what great things God has done for you. It is good that you have been healed; it will be better if someone turns to Christ because of your deliverance.

If you have not experienced a miracle, you have missed something somewhere. Start over. And over.

And over. Your Heavenly Father loves you. And He will either heal you or give you an experience that will transcend healing. Consider each of these 10 instructions slowly, prayerfully, and humbly. God has a miracle for you!

"Bless the Lord, O my soul: and all that is within me, bless his holy name. Bless the Lord, O my soul, and forget not all his benefits: who forgiveth all thine iniquities; who healeth all thy diseases" (Psalm 103:1-3).